What Is
the Panama Canal?

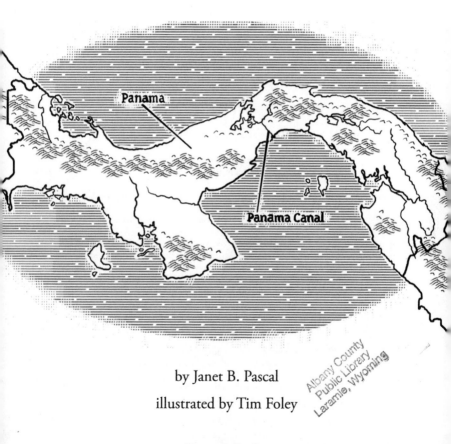

Panama

Panama Canal

by Janet B. Pascal

illustrated by Tim Foley

Grosset & Dunlap
An Imprint of Penguin Group (USA) LLC

For Gerard Mancini, who manages an operation
even more complex than the Panama Canal—JBP

GROSSET & DUNLAP
Published by the Penguin Group
Penguin Group (USA) LLC, 375 Hudson Street, New York, New York 10014, USA

USA | Canada | UK | Ireland | Australia | New Zealand | India | South Africa | China

penguin.com
A Penguin Random House Company

Text copyright © 2014 by Janet B. Pascal. Illustrations copyright © 2014 by Penguin
Group (USA) LLC. All rights reserved. Published by Grosset & Dunlap, a division
of Penguin Young Readers Group, 345 Hudson Street, New York, New York 10014.
GROSSET & DUNLAP is a trademark of Penguin Group (USA) LLC.
Printed in the USA.

Library of Congress Cataloging-in-Publication Data is available.

ISBN 978-0-448-47899-9   10 9 8 7 6 5 4 3

Contents

North
America

Atlantic
Ocean

Panama

Pacific
Ocean

South
America

Cape Horn

Antarctica

What Is the Panama Canal?

"I would never . . . navigate . . . round that wretched place again. It is the kingdom of Satan," said a sailor in the nineteenth century. He was speaking of the trip around Cape Horn between South America and Antarctica. "Rounding the Horn," as sailors call it, is one of the wildest, most dangerous trips a ship can make. For as many as two hundred days a year, gale-force winds blow there with gusts ranging from fifty to eighty miles per hour. The waves can reach ninety feet high or more.

Yet for hundreds of years, if anyone wanted to sail west from the Atlantic to the Pacific Ocean, they had no choice. They had to round the Horn. Surviving the trip became the sign of a truly brave seaman. After a sailor had managed to sail around the Horn three times, he could wear a silver earring, as a badge of honor. Many did not make it. No one knows for sure, but there may be one thousand shipwrecks lying under the water, and as many as fifteen thousand drowned sailors.

People dreamed of an easier way to sail from the Atlantic to the Pacific Ocean. On maps, one place looked very promising. This was the Isthmus of Panama. An isthmus is a narrow strip connecting two pieces of land. The Isthmus of Panama joins Central America to South America. On one side is the Caribbean Sea, which runs into the Atlantic Ocean. On the other, the Gulf of Panama flows into the Pacific. At its narrowest, the isthmus is only thirty miles wide. The Atlantic and the Pacific looked so close together there! Surely some way could be found to cut across. Then ships would be able to sail right through Panama. The trip would become thousands of miles shorter,

and no one would have to risk their lives sailing around Cape Horn.

The reality was much more complicated than the dream. Panama was narrow, but it was rough and dangerous, with jungles, swamps, rivers, and high mountains in the way. It took years of work and failure before a passageway through was finally cut. Fortunes were won and lost. Thousands of people died. A revolution even had to be fought.

Gulf of Panama

South America

Pacific Ocean

Finally the United States of America made the dream come true. On August 15, 1914, the first ship sailed through the Panama Canal from one ocean to the other. World travel would never be the same again.

CHAPTER 1
From the Atlantic to the Pacific

The first European to see the Pacific Ocean from the Americas was the Spanish explorer Vasco Núñez de Balboa. In 1513, he was governor of a

Spanish province in Panama. The local Indians told him about a place where, if he hiked only a short distance, he could see the ocean on the other side. So he took a small party of men and set out through the jungle and up the mountains. He made all his men stay behind him, to make sure that *he* would see the ocean first. On

September 25, from the top of a mountain range, he spotted the Pacific Ocean in the distance.

A few years later, in 1534, King Charles I of Spain sent an expedition to find out if it would be possible to create a way through Panama by water. However, the expedition decided it was impossible. Instead the Spanish used two narrow roads cut through the isthmus. They ran through

thick jungles and swamps.
In places, travelers had
to crawl on their hands
and knees through
deep, sticky mud. The
Spanish used these roads
to bring back gold and
treasure taken from the Indians.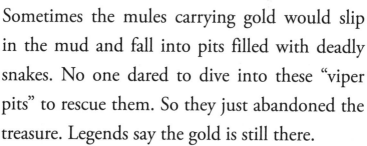
Sometimes the mules carrying gold would slip
in the mud and fall into pits filled with deadly
snakes. No one dared to dive into these "viper
pits" to rescue them. So they just abandoned the
treasure. Legends say the gold is still there.

In 1848, gold was discovered in California. By 1849, eager gold seekers called "forty-niners" were racing to California, hoping to strike it rich. They came from all over the world. Miners all wanted to stake a claim to the gold before someone else beat them to it. So getting from the East Coast of America to the West Coast as fast as possible was vital.

For the first time in centuries, there was a lot of interest in the path across Panama. Traveling by land across North America to California in a covered wagon took months. Ships were faster. But the journey from New York to California by sea was 17,000 miles. Even on a fast ship, the trip would take three to five months. The journey from New York to Panama was only 2,000 miles. That trip took two weeks. The 3,500 miles from the other side of the isthmus to San Francisco took about three weeks more. And if you crossed Panama using the old Spanish roads, there were only forty-seven miles to go on foot—how long could that take? Using a shortcut through Panama could cut the trip to less than half the time it took to round Cape Horn.

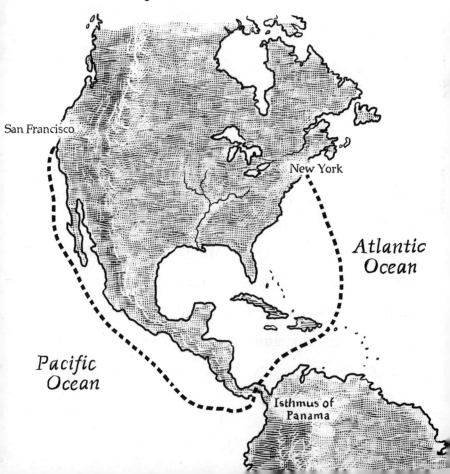

Suddenly Panama was overrun with hopeful
gold miners trying to cross on foot. They
discovered that the hike was worse than any
nightmare. They waded through mud up to their
waists. The jungle was so thick that often they
could see only a few feet ahead. The paths were so
narrow that sometimes a mule got stuck between
trees or rocks. Everywhere lay the rotting corpses

of mules that had died. There were poisonous snakes, scorpions, spiders, and mosquitoes. It was not possible to travel much faster than a mile an hour, so the trip could take a week. People had to sleep outside on the ground, even during thunderstorms when the water came down in solid sheets.

Worst of all were the fevers. Everyone who traveled to Panama seemed to get sick. A man could be perfectly healthy when he started the hike across. A few days later he might be dead. "In fear of God and the love of man . . . for no consideration come this route," advised one man who survived it. And yet people wanted to get to all that gold in California. The hordes kept coming.

CHAPTER 2
A Railroad Built on Corpses

Even before the forty-niners, the dream of building a waterway across Panama had never been completely forgotten. But everyone who had ever looked into it had given up. It seemed impossible. The United States of America was especially interested. Americans were sure their country would soon stretch all the way across the continent to the Pacific Ocean. Once it did, the different parts of the country would need a way to send mail, ship goods, and communicate between the East and West Coasts.

Land travel was difficult. Thousands of miles of wilderness still separated the coasts. So a way for ships to cross at Panama would be particularly useful for Americans.

After 1821, Panama was no longer under Spanish control. It became part of the South American country that would eventually be known as Colombia. Many people in Panama wanted to separate and form their own country. In 1846, the United States signed a treaty with Colombia. The United States promised that if Panama tried to break away, it would support Colombia against the rebels. In return, Colombia gave the United States the right to build either a canal or a railroad over the isthmus.

In 1850 a private American company called the Panama Railroad Company was created to build a railroad across Panama. Every step of building a railroad turned out to be much harder than anyone had imagined. The first eight miles had to be laid

on swampland. To create a firm bed for the railroad, workers tried to fill in the swamps with gravel. But the mud seemed to be bottomless. No matter how much gravel was poured in, everything kept sinking. Some places needed as much as two hundred feet of gravel before building could be started. Then the rainy season came. Heavy rain fell almost every day. Places the builders had filled in turned back to mud and had to be filled in all over again.

A lot of the work had to be done by hand, using picks and shovels. A huge workforce was needed. Laborers poured into Panama from all over the world. Unfortunately, Panama seemed to be one of the unhealthiest places on earth. As fast as workers came, they caught tropical fevers and died. So many people died that it became a problem figuring out what to do with all the bodies. Many of the dead were poor people with no families to claim them. The company found a way to make money out of them. Medical students always needed more corpses to study, so the Panama Railroad Company began to ship corpses, pickled in barrels, to medical schools all over the world.

For a while, it seemed that the job was too

hard. The company almost failed. But finally, on January 27, 1855, the railroad was finished. It had taken five years and cost millions of dollars more than expected. There were no good records, so no one knew exactly how many people had died during construction. Estimates range from five thousand to twelve thousand. According to Mark Twain, "Every railroad tie . . . rests upon a corpse."

The railroad was "a wonderful triumph of man's indomitable will over the hostile powers of nature," wrote one journalist. By 1856, it was carrying an average of forty thousand people a year. Because travelers had no other choice, the company could charge as much as it liked. The first-class price for the forty-seven-mile trip was $25 per person, plus extra for baggage. That was a lot of money at a time when a working man might earn only a dollar a day.

Crossing Panama by railroad was a lot more fun than walking. One early traveler called the railroad trip "one of the most delightful rides I ever enjoyed, through the rich tropical scenery of the Isthmus."

The success of the railroad brought the dream of building a canal back to life. Of course, building a canal is more complicated than building a railroad. A train can climb steep hills. A ship needs a flat path. How could anyone dig a canal

all the way through the mountains of Panama? A train can cross a river by going over a bridge. A ship can't. The powerful Chagres River ran right over any possible path across Panama. Digging a canal through it would create a giant waterfall.

The jungles, swamps, and mountains of Panama were so thick and wild that no one had a good idea what the land was really like. Many people hoped that somewhere, still hidden, might lie the perfect path for a canal. Between 1870 and 1875, the United States sent seven different teams to explore places where a canal could perhaps be built. These expeditions had a miserable time. Mosquitoes and biting insects were so thick they kept everyone awake at night. Sudden rainstorms caused such terrible flooding that the explorers sometimes had to spend the night roosting in the trees. One man said it was "the worst country I ever saw."

All the exploration seemed to show that building a canal across Panama was impossible. A better place to build might be Nicaragua, farther north. The distance across Nicaragua was more than three times longer than at Panama. But the mountains were lower. The land was more open. And at Nicaragua, there was a huge lake that could be used as part of the canal.

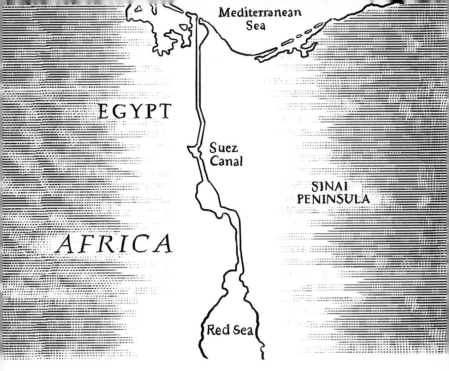

Canal building became a hot topic after 1869. That year, the Suez Canal was opened. This canal cut across Egypt for about one hundred miles to join the Mediterranean Sea with the Red Sea. Ships could now sail from Europe to Asia without having to go all the way around Africa. Many people had believed this project was impossible, yet it was successfully completed. If a Suez Canal was possible, why not a Panama Canal?

The main force behind the Suez Canal was a Frenchman named Ferdinand de Lesseps. He was a dashing and handsome man of great energy and charm. He believed he could succeed at anything he wanted. More important, he had the gift of making other people believe in him. Once the Suez Canal was finished, he turned his attention to the idea of a canal across Central America.

CHAPTER 3
A Canal?

In 1875, a group of scientists, explorers, engineers, and politicians from all over the world, headed by de Lesseps, met in France to figure out if it was possible to build a canal across Central America. There were two possible kinds of canal

they considered. The canal could be dug entirely at sea level. The builders would dig down as deep as needed to make a flat channel from the Atlantic to the Pacific Oceans. Ships would be able to sail in one end, across, and out the other. Or the canal could be built using locks. Locks are a kind of water ladder used to raise ships up and down. Instead of having to dig all the way to sea level, the builders would create a canal higher up. One set of locks would lift ships up to the height of the land being crossed. Then the ship would sail across. At the other end, another set of locks would lower it back down to sea level.

The group decided that a canal should be built through Nicaragua, using locks. Then de Lesseps stepped in and told the others they were all wrong. The plan, he said, was much too complicated. The canal must be built at sea level, as the Suez Canal had been. And it should be built through Panama, not Nicaragua. Certainly there were difficulties to be overcome. But when a problem had come up at Suez, he had always found a solution. He was sure that if he was in charge of a new company, he could get the job done in Panama, as well. De Lesseps was very convincing. After all, he was the most successful canal builder ever. A private group, with de Lesseps at the head, was formed to raise money and build the canal.

De Lesseps got permission from the Colombian government for the company to dig a canal through Panama. The directors of the Panama Canal Company also had to figure out how to deal with the Panama railroad, which ran over the same path the canal would follow. They decided it would be simplest just to buy the railroad from its American owners. The trains could be very useful during the building process.

Of course all this would cost a lot. The company set to work raising money. People could buy shares in the Panama Canal Company, with

the promise of becoming very rich once the canal opened. But if the company failed, the investors would lose their money. Most of the money came from France, because de Lesseps was a hero to the French people. When he promised them the canal would be built, they believed him.

CHAPTER 4
The French Try Their Hand

Triumphantly, de Lesseps set sail for Panama. He had promised his investors that the first shovelful of earth for the canal would be dug on January 1, 1880, at the Pacific entrance. On the day of the ceremony, however, the boat set out

too late. The tide had already turned. They were not able to get anywhere near the site. So instead, de Lesseps had his small daughter, Ferdinande, turn over some sand in a box on board the boat. This ceremony, sadly, was a sign of how the entire building effort would go.

Real work started soon afterward. Since no one had ever done what the builders were doing now, they worked by trial and error. No one knew exactly what machines were needed or how they would be used. Soon the site was littered with abandoned machines that hadn't worked out. Giant steam excavators turned out to be the best way to dig. These were a kind of railroad car with what looked like a long ladder hanging off the side. Each rung of the ladder held a chain of buckets that would lift earth up to the top of the hole. There it would be loaded on railway cars that hauled it away.

De Lesseps had great faith in his engineers, and in new technology. He told people that the Panama Canal would be easier to build than the Suez Canal. However, the Suez Canal had been dug in dry, flat sand. The Panama site was nothing like that. There were so many different kinds of dirt, mud, and rock that a team never knew beforehand what they would be digging in.

Each kind of soil had its own problems. The worst was the heavy blue and green clay. It stuck to shovels and the buckets of the steam excavators. Workers had to stop and knock it off by hand. In some places, the land was so steep, the machinery had to balance on narrow, flat spaces carved out of the hillside. If the ground was soft, huge machines would fall over into the holes they were digging.

The rainy season made everything much worse. During the months of May to November, twenty inches of rain or more could fall in a month. If the earth wasn't taken away quickly enough, a sudden storm could wash it all right back into the channel it had been dug out of. Heavy rainfall could make a muddy hillside slide down into the excavation, covering over train tracks or machinery.

To prevent landslides, the engineers had to keep making the canal wider. They had to dig deeper and deeper into the sides of steep hills. They soon realized they would have to dig out many times more dirt than they had thought. This meant a lot more work—and money—than they had predicted.

Another huge problem was the Chagres River. It ran right across any possible path the canal could take, and it was high above sea level. In order for the canal to be dug down to sea level, some way would have to be found to move the river. No one knew how to send a powerful river to a totally different place. De Lesseps wasn't worried. He was sure one of his brilliant engineers would figure out how—eventually.

Worst of all was the problem that plagued everyone in Panama—disease. About twenty thousand men a year were needed to keep the work going. But as fast as workers were shipped in, they caught malaria or yellow fever and died. Sometimes as many as forty people died in a day.

The general belief was that bad air from the swamps caused the fevers. Filthy living conditions were also blamed. Many Europeans truly believed

that if they lived clean, healthy lives, they would not get sick. To prove it, Jules Dingler, one of the chief French engineers, brought his wife, son, daughter-in-law, and future son-in-law out to Panama to live with him. "I am going to show them that only drunkards and the dissipated contract yellow fever and die," he declared. He was wrong. Soon all four of his family members were dead. Dingler himself survived to go back to France, where he died brokenhearted a few years later.

No one knows exactly how many people died from diseases during the nine years the French were in Panama. The best guess is somewhere between twenty and twenty-two thousand.

The French kept on bravely against all odds. De Lesseps was still sure that everything would work out. Several times the company went back to its stockholders to raise more money. After seven years, no more than about one-tenth of the canal had been dug. And there was still no plan to deal with the Chagres River.

In May 1889, the company went bankrupt. Company officials were accused of stealing huge sums of money and of bribing high-level French politicians. They were hauled into court in France. The trial dragged on until 1893. De Lesseps was by now in his late eighties. He did not have to go

to court and never really knew what was going on. He died in 1894. However, his son Charles, who had worked with him, served time in jail. The dream had ended in disaster.

CHAPTER 5
The United States Steps In

The United States had never lost interest in a canal across Central America, even though trains had made crossing North America much easier. In 1869, a railroad had finally been built that connected the East Coast with the West Coast.

But it was still easier to ship large quantities of heavy things by boat than by train. And boats still had to go all the way around the Horn. As a strong, rich, and growing nation, with cities on both coasts of North America, the United States had more to gain than any other country from a canal that would provide a shortcut.

Building the Transcontinental Railroad

In 1863, the United States government began building a railroad that would cross the entire continent, a distance of three thousand miles. Two companies worked on the railroad. One started in California. The other started in Iowa, where it could hook up with eastern railroads that already existed. On May 10, 1869, the two sections met up in Utah. Now it was possible to travel from coast to coast in about a week. However, the new railroad didn't mean the Panama Canal was no longer needed. Since the tracks went over mountain passes and through tunnels, they couldn't carry the huge amount of heavy freight a ship could.

In 1901, Theodore Roosevelt became president of the United States. He was, in some ways, similar to Ferdinand de Lesseps. He was confident and energetic. When he believed in something, he pushed ahead. He knew how to make other people believe in him.

Roosevelt thought a canal was important. But he believed that it should be built in Nicaragua. He said the French failure proved that Panama was a bad choice.

The French, however, desperately wanted the United States to buy out their company. So they needed to convince the United States to build in Panama. They offered to sell the company for less than half its worth. This was a real bargain. The French had already started eleven miles of canal. Blasting had lowered the height of the mountains that ran across the middle of isthmus. The railroad was there. All the company's buildings, machinery, supplies, and equipment were still on the site. And the French company hinted that if the United States wasn't interested, some other country might be. Maybe Germany, which was trying to become a military power. The United States certainly wouldn't want that to happen.

Roosevelt changed his mind, and in June 1902 the United States Congress voted to build a canal in Panama.

CHAPTER 6
War!

Until now, only private companies had been interested in building a canal. Their main goal was to make money. Any ship, from any country, would be able to use the canal as long as it was willing to pay. Roosevelt's ideas were a little different. He was interested in the canal's military usefulness. He believed it should be built and controlled by the United States government. In times of peace, any ship could use it. But if the United States was at war, he wanted to be able to keep its enemies out of the canal.

Before the canal could be built, Roosevelt had to work out a treaty between the United States and Colombia. And that wasn't easy.

Roosevelt said Colombia had to give the United States control of the area around the canal. The US should be able to build military bases there and run it as if it was part of the United States. Not surprisingly, the Colombian government didn't want to give away so much power. It began to look as if the two countries would never agree.

According to international law, one country can't just start a revolution in another country. The United States couldn't tell Colombia, "If you won't let us dig in Panama, then we'll turn Panama into an independent country." But that is basically what happened.

Officially, the United States government wasn't involved. The revolution was planned by private supporters of the Panama Canal, led by a Frenchman named Philippe Bunau-Varilla. If

Philippe Bunau-Varilla

there were talks with American politicians, they happened in secret. But most people believe that the US government knew what was going on and approved. Starting the revolution wasn't very hard. Panamanians had been fighting to separate from Colombia for years. Bunau-Varilla convinced a Panamanian patriot named Manuel Amador that if he led a revolution, he would have the support of the United States. Amador agreed.

Manuel Amador

The date of the Panamanian revolution was set for November 3, 1903. It was almost comically easy. Since people thought the United States was behind him, Amador had no trouble getting them to fight on his side. There were only a few Colombian soldiers stationed at Panama. They quickly agreed to switch sides.

A United States gunship, the USS *Nashville*, was sent down to Panama to see what was going on. It just sat in the harbor. Still, the sight of an American gunship was enough. Colombia gave up. The entire revolution lasted only a few hours. Only one shopkeeper and a donkey were killed.

On November 6, 1903, the United States officially recognized the new republic of Panama. (Colombia didn't recognize Panama until 1921.)

Now Roosevelt sent gunboats down to help Panama. The message to Colombia was clear: Whether or not the United States had caused this revolution, it would defend the new country now that it existed.

The treaty between the United States and the new country of Panama gave the United States exactly what it wanted. It created a zone ten miles wide where the canal would be built. The United States would not own this land. Officially it was still part of Panama. But the US would be able to act exactly as if the land belonged to it. The government of Panama would have no power there. Most important, the treaty said that US control of the canal zone would never end. It would last "in perpetuity"—forever.

People all over the world accused Roosevelt of acting like a bully. But he didn't care. He believed in using all the power he had as president to fight for what he thought was right. And he didn't make threats he wasn't prepared to back up. In Panama, he used the United States Navy to follow his favorite proverb: "Speak softly and carry a big stick."

CHAPTER 7
Killing Mosquitoes

Most Americans were sure that their country would have less trouble in Panama than the French had. "I should say that the building of the canal will be a comparatively easy task for knowing, enterprising, and energetic Americans," one journalist wrote. Within a few months, several thousand workers had arrived in Panama.

They moved into the rotting French work camps, cleaned up the rusty machinery, and picked up right where the French had left off.

"Make the dirt fly!" Roosevelt told his chief engineer. And so the workers plunged in and started digging. They didn't know exactly what they were supposed to be doing. The final plans for the canal were still not settled. So they just went ahead blindly. They thought they could work out problems as they went along. It looked as if the Americans were repeating all the mistakes the French had made. Roosevelt soon realized that this wouldn't work. They needed to step back and take the time to figure out how to do the job right.

Clearly the first thing to do was to conquer disease. No huge project could succeed if all the workers kept dying. By now, scientists were realizing that mosquitoes might be the key. In 1897 Ronald Ross had been able to prove that

malaria was spread by a specific kind of mosquito. By 1900, research by Carlos Finlay and Walter Reed had led to the same discovery about yellow fever.

Malaria and Yellow Fever

Malaria and yellow fever are very different diseases, spread by two different kinds of mosquitoes.

A person with malaria suffers from high fever and headaches. Most eventually recover. But sometimes the disease might come back years later and kill them. In the seventeenth century, it was discovered that quinine from the bark of a South American tree could help treat malaria. But nothing could prevent it. Even today, there is no vaccine to prevent people from catching it. It still kills as many as one million people a year, mostly in tropical countries.

Yellow fever causes vomiting and pain. If it damages the liver, the sick person might turn yellow. Almost one-sixth of the people who catch it die. There is now a vaccine to keep people from getting yellow fever, but there is still no good way to cure it.

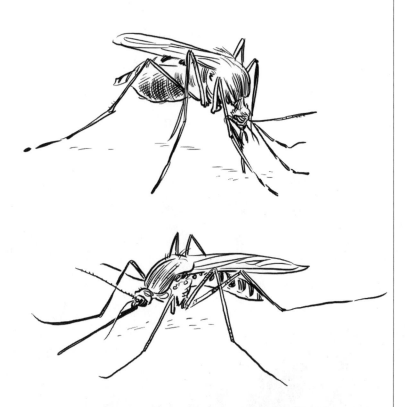

Doctors were finally able to prove that
mosquitoes caused these diseases. Their pioneering
work was made possible by brave volunteers. These
people let mosquitoes bite them so they could see if
they got sick. Many of the volunteers caught yellow
fever or malaria, and some died.

The French hadn't known that fevers were carried by mosquitoes. So purely by accident, they had made the spread of disease much worse. Digging the canal had created a paradise for mosquitoes, since they breed in pools of standing water. Unfortunately, the construction sites had created hundreds of these pools.

The French had also built a large hospital to take care of the sick. To protect the patients from crawling bugs, the feet of beds stood in bowls of water. This, too, attracted mosquitoes. In fact, the hospital had so many mosquitoes that if a patient didn't have malaria or yellow fever when he went in, he would probably catch it while he was there.

Unfortunately most ordinary people still thought the idea that mosquitoes could make people sick sounded silly. Colonel William Gorgas became Panama's chief medical officer. He had already helped end yellow fever in Havana, Cuba, by killing all the mosquitoes there. In Panama, he hoped to do the same thing. But it would take a lot of work, and he would need a lot of money— maybe as much as $1,000,000. He was afraid no one would listen to him. What if they thought it was too much trouble and expense just to get rid of some bugs?

Roosevelt didn't like wasting time or money, but he wanted results. He asked a doctor friend for advice. Was killing mosquitoes really worth the effort? "If you fall back on the old methods of sanitation, you will fail, just as the French failed," the doctor told him. "If you back up Gorgas . . . you will get your canal." Roosevelt gave Gorgas everything he needed.

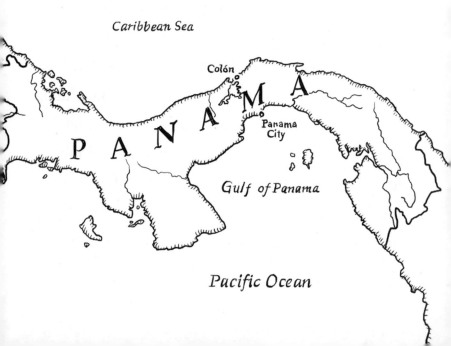

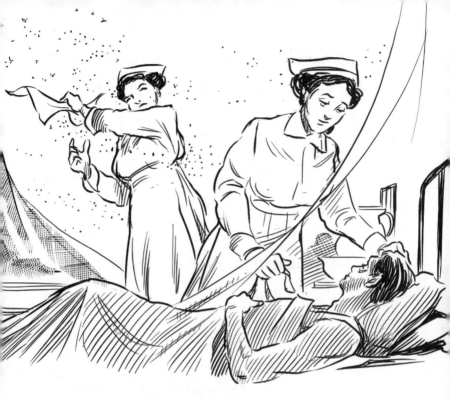

It was not a simple problem to solve. Havana
had been only one city. At Panama, there were two
main cities, Panama City and Colón, separated
by miles of swamps and jungle and a canal in
progress. And there were a *lot* of mosquitoes. They
were so thick they snuffed out candles at night. In
the hospital, nurses had to work in teams, one to
tend a patient, and one to chase mosquitoes away.

The Panama treaty had given the United States complete control over all health measures in the canal zone. Gorgas's crews forced the people of Panama to live in ways that would prevent mosquitoes from breeding. No one was allowed to keep drinking water in uncovered pitchers. Instead, American engineers installed running water and a modern sewage system in the two cities. Gorgas's men even went into churches

and cleaned out holy-water fonts. They searched every home. If they found mosquitoes, carpenters were sent in to rebuild all the places where water might collect. They used insect-killing chemicals anywhere someone had died of yellow fever.

Outside the cities, there was even more work to do. Miles of jungle land had to be treated so there would be nowhere for mosquitoes to breed. Teams of men working for Gorgas filled in swamps. They paved roads and dug drainage ditches. They covered standing pools with a thin film of oil that kept mosquitoes from laying their eggs.

It was a huge job. But it worked. Malaria became rare. Only a few people died a year, instead of thousands. Yellow fever was even more of a success story. In 1906, only two years after Gorgas began his program, there was only one case of yellow fever. After that, there was not one single case of the disease during the entire time the canal was being built.

CHAPTER 8
A Man with a Plan

The United States' first year in Panama was discouraging. Millions were spent, but the canal was no further along. In 1905, things began to turn around. The original chief engineer was replaced by John Stevens.

Stevens understood how to run a large-scale project. He had spent his life helping build the great railroads that crossed the North American continent. When he took over the canal project, he was brave enough to put a stop to the digging. He realized there was no point in going ahead until a plan was worked out and all the important questions were settled.

With the digging on hold, Stevens used the time to deal with the problem of housing and feeding the workers. There was no good place for them to live. The French had left behind work camps that were airless, damp, and full of bugs and rats. Food had to be bought from local merchants. It was very expensive, and often spoiled or moldy. Stevens realized that he needed to attract intelligent, hard workers. The kind of people he wanted wouldn't be willing to stay unless he could offer them a pleasant place to live. So he had the construction crews build dry, comfortable

housing for the workers, with baseball diamonds, schools, dance halls, and theaters, so there would be something to do after hours. The new towns along the canal zone would not have looked out of place in New Jersey. Special canal zone stores sold food sent down from the United States, for much lower prices than the Panamanian stores. Only Panama Canal workers could shop at them.

The Culebra Cut

Workers using machetes to clear the jungle in the canal zone

A steam shovel loading dirt onto railroad cars

Abandoned French machinery on a bank of the canal

SUMMARY OF ROUTES.

Names of Routes.	Length.	Cost.
1. The Wyse Panama Route	45 miles and 1,986 feet.	$140,000,000
2. The Nicaragua Route	181 miles and 2,664 feet.	180,400,000
3. San Blas Route	34 miles and 4,426 feet.	268,000,000
4. Atrato Napipi, or the Cupica Route..	180 miles and 1,380 feet.	206,000,000
5. Tiati-Tolo Route.....................	78 miles	120,000,000
6. Tuyra-Caquirri Route................	145 miles	130,000,000

7. Truando Atrato Route—mainly corresponding with Route No. 4.

Should the Canal be constructed as proposed, as it ultimately must be, the distance from New York to San Francisco, for ships, will be reduced by 14,000 miles; to Shanghai, 11,690 miles; to Canton, 10,900 miles; and to Calcutta, 9,000 miles. It is estimated that this diminution of the sea voyage by the use of the Canal would result in a saving of at least $36,000,000 annually to the trade of the United States.

An early map of potential Panama Canal routes

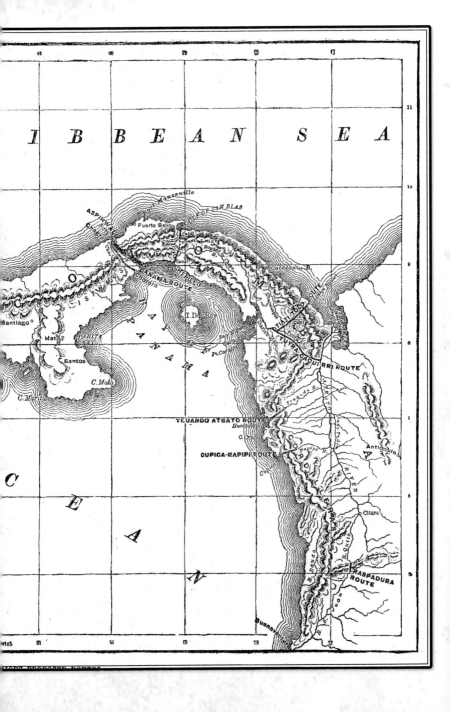

Ferdinand de Lesseps with his wife and nine of his children

Canal workers

A landslide completely blocking the canal

Two workers cooking a meal

Hotel Tivoli, which provided housing for canal workers

Workers prepare to blast with dynamite

President Theodore Roosevelt running
an American steam shovel at the Culebra Cut

Gatun Dam and the south lake entrance to the locks

Colonel William Gorgas at a building site for the Panama Canal

A man spraying
oil on mosquito-
breeding areas

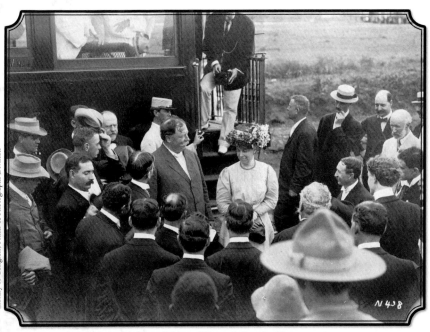

President Taft and his wife arriving in Panama in 1907

Gatun Dam spillway in Panama

A crowd at the opening ceremony of the Panama Canal

The SS *Ancon* on the Panama Canal's opening day, August 15, 1914

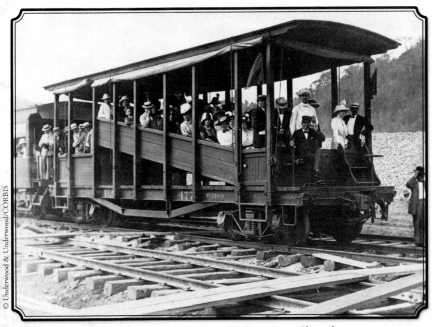

A sightseeing car on the Panama railroad

American tourists posing in front of one of the gates of the canal

Anniversary celebration at Gatun Locks in 1939

President Theodore Roosevelt

A warship and a tanker at a lock

The main operations room for the Gatun Locks

A modern aerial view of the Panama Canal

Racism

Racial discrimination was everywhere in the canal zone. Workers were put on the "gold roll" or the "silver roll," according to whether they were paid in gold or silver. This was supposed to reflect the kind of work they did. The gold roll was supposed to be for skilled workers. The silver roll was meant for those who did basic physical labor. Actually, the rolls were used to enforce segregation. Most gold-roll workers were American citizens, and almost all were white. Silver-roll workers usually came from the Caribbean and Latin America and were black or Hispanic. But even blacks who held skilled jobs and were American citizens usually found themselves on the silver roll.

Silver-roll workers were not just paid less. The new houses and villages built by the Panama Canal Company were only for gold-roll people. Those on the silver roll had to find their own housing or live in rundown old barracks. Most of them crowded into tiny rooms in the cities or set up camp in the jungle. Since they lived outside the areas protected from mosquitoes, many more nonwhites than whites died from disease.

In 1906, Stevens finally felt ready to let the digging start again. At last a definite plan for the canal had been approved. Until now, it had never been completely settled whether the canal would have locks or not. Many people still wanted it to be built at sea level. Now the US Senate and President Roosevelt decided, once and for all. They would not try to dig a canal at sea level. They would build a raised canal, using locks.

When the digging started up again, Stevens did something no one before him had: He worked out a complete system that would keep construction running at full speed. He understood that the

railroad could be used in much better ways that anyone had done so far.

The French had sometimes left the dirt they dug out sitting by the side of the canal for days. Not only did it get in the way of workers, when it rained, the dirt washed right back into the hole it had been dug from. And when they were ready to haul it away, often no railroad cars were available.

Stevens understood that the entire operation had to work like a watch, with every piece always in the right place at the right time. He bought the best steam shovels available, and figured out how much dirt they could dig per hour. Then

he rebuilt the railroad so he could run an endless stream of cars to and from the diggers. As soon as one car was filled, it moved on, and another one moved into its place. The dirt was taken away to places where it would be needed for construction later.

The canal plan that was finally settled on called for building a dam across the Chagres River. Before this, the river had been a problem. The new plan turned it into an advantage. The dammed-up

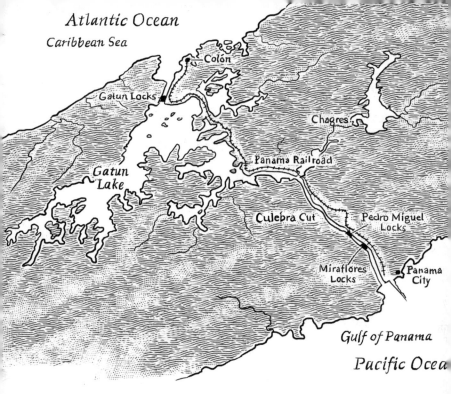

waters would form a long artificial lake called Gatun Lake that would become part of the canal. When ships entered the canal from the Atlantic Ocean, a set of three locks would lift them up eighty-five feet above sea level. They would travel twenty-three miles across the artificial lake and through a nine-mile-long waterway, today called the Culebra Cut, that workers would have to blast through the mountain ridge that ran down the middle of Panama. Three more locks would lower the ships on the other side. A three-mile-long breakwater at the Pacific end would help deal with the extreme ocean tides. It was an excellent plan, one that had already been proposed by a French engineer thirty-one years ago. But back then, no one had been interested.

Theodore Roosevelt was eager to go out and see how his canal was coming along. Every other government figure had traveled to Panama during the dry season, when the weather was pleasant. But Roosevelt went at the height of the rainy season. And he had a wonderful time. He was photographed working one of the giant steam shovels Stevens had bought. The picture appeared all over the United States and helped make the Panama Canal popular with ordinary citizens. Finally everything was going well.

CHAPTER 9
Finishing the Job

Then suddenly, in January 1907, Stevens quit. He never explained why, and no one ever found out. He may simply have been exhausted— he had done a huge amount of work in just a few years. Roosevelt was furious. He had liked Stevens, and now he felt betrayed. So for the last head engineer, the man who would take the canal to completion, he chose a military man, Colonel George Washington Goethals. A soldier, Roosevelt believed, would never desert his post.

Goethals took over a well-run, efficient operation. Wisely, he did not try to change things that were already working. He concentrated on keeping morale high and making operations simpler. Still, even with everything going

smoothly, no one could say Goethals had an easy job. The men were trying to move more dirt and rock than anyone had ever done before and to create the largest artificial lake ever, in a brutally difficult climate. What's more, once they had created the lake it would flood the site of the old railroad, so most of the railroad would have to be rebuilt somewhere else.

For Goethals there were three big engineering problems to be conquered. First was the Culebra Cut. For nine miles, the path of the canal had to be carved 150 feet down through the solid rock of the mountains. Work on the cut went on day and night, with digging during the day, and dynamite and cleanup work at night. About 160 trainloads of dirt and rock were removed every day. It was extremely dangerous work—despite safety precautions, many men were blown up.

The ground was unstable. Constant blasting made it worse. Sometimes huge slides would fill in a section of the cut. Machines were buried, and days of work were lost. There was nothing to be done about this, and Goethals stayed calm. After a very bad slide filled in a section of the cut completely, the engineer in charge came to

him in shock, asking what to do. Goethals simply said, "Dig it out again." The landslides have never stopped completely. Even now, sometimes there will be a slide, and a segment of the Culebra Cut will need to be dredged out.

The Culebra Cut was the part of the work that most fascinated the world. It became a tourist attraction. As many as twenty thousand Americans a year came out to stand on a mountain ridge high above the cut, watching the men at work.

After all the discussion, damming the Chagres River to create Gatun Lake turned out to be surprisingly easy. A narrow valley with high hills on both sides proved an ideal location. The main problem was that the dam had to be so huge. At its base, it was half a mile wide. It was over a mile and a quarter long, and 105 feet high. This took a lot of earth to build. But the engineers were removing more than enough material from the Culebra Cut. It was relatively simple to send it by train to the site of the dam and dump it there. As an added benefit, the dam would operate a hydroelectric power plant. This would generate all the electricity needed to run the locks.

In October 1913, President Woodrow Wilson, who was in Washington, DC, pushed a specially built button. Thousands of miles away in Panama, this set off a charge of dynamite. The newly created Gatun Lake was joined to the Culebra Cut.

CHAPTER 10
Success!

Building the locks was the last challenge before the canal could open. A lot had been learned in the twenty years since the French had first tried to design locks for Panama. Many of the engineers working there now had helped build and run locks in the Great Lakes. Still, designing the locks was a huge task, because, like the dam, they needed to be so big.

At each end of the canal, there were three stages of locks. And since the canal would be carrying so much traffic going in both directions, all the locks were made with double chambers, so that more than one ship could travel at a time. That made twelve chambers in all. They were designed to be large enough to hold even the greatest

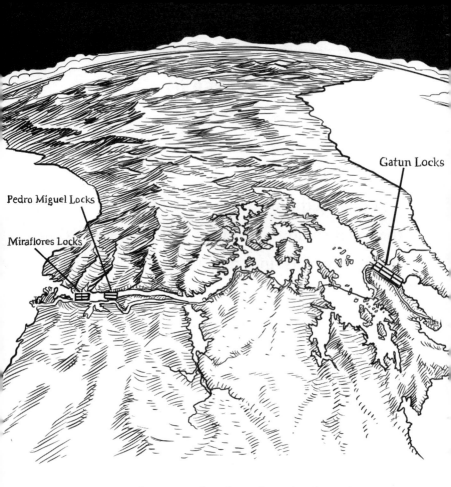

Gatun Locks

Pedro Miguel Locks

Miraflores Locks

oceangoing ship. Each chamber had to be over
1,000 feet long and 110 feet wide. Nothing so
huge had ever been made of concrete before, and
special new ways had to be invented to pour the
concrete.

How Locks Work

Locks lift or lower ships from a pool of water at one level to a pool at another level. A set of locks consists of a series of basins, each one higher than the one before. The basins have high walls and gates at each end. When a ship needs to be raised, the back gate of the lowest basin is opened. The ship sails in, and the gate is closed. Then water is poured into the basin. The ship floats up as the water level rises. When the ship is as high as the next basin, the gate at the front end of the basin is opened. Then the ship sails into the higher basin. The reverse is done for a ship that needs to be lowered.

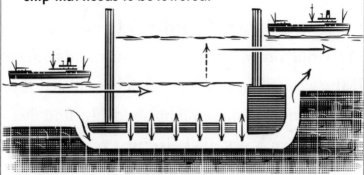

The locks were operated from a central control room with a miniature model of the entire canal. Each part of the model moved, so that it perfectly matched its position in the actual canal.

If the steps for working the locks were done in the wrong order, terrible accidents could happen. If the wrong end of a lock chamber opened first, for instance, a ship might suddenly find itself riding down a waterfall. To prevent this, all the switches were designed so they would open and close only in the right order.

Work on the three parts of the canal went on for seven years, under three US presidents: Theodore Roosevelt, William Taft, and Woodrow Wilson. At last, on October 10, 1913, a complete, unbroken water pathway from ocean to ocean was completed.

Theodore Roosevelt

William Taft

On January 7, 1914, before the canal opened, a construction boat, the *Alexandre La Valley*, became the first ship to travel from one end to the other. The first ship to sail through

Woodrow Wilson

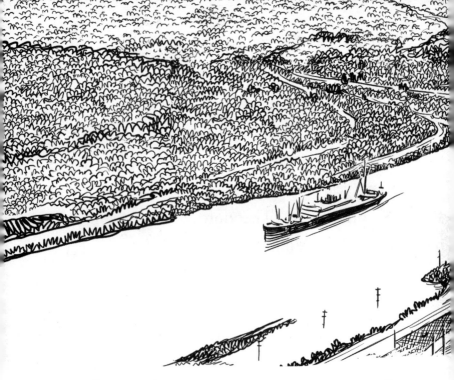

officially was the SS *Ancon*, on August 15. After
spending ten years and $400 million, the United
States had finally succeeded.

Huge celebrations had been planned, with
fleets of ships coming down to Panama from
both sides of the continent. But fate intervened.
At the beginning of August, Germany declared
war on Russia, France, and Belgium, and World

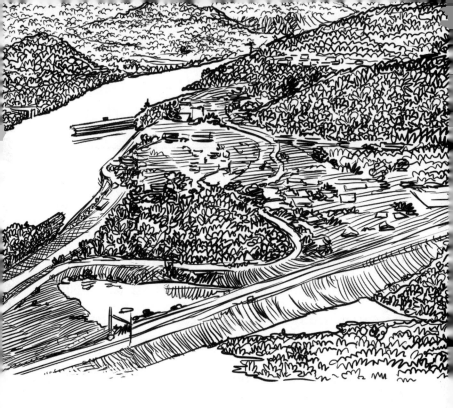

War I began. All celebrations at Panama were cancelled. Still, not even a war could lessen what had been achieved. Four hundred and one years after Balboa first crossed the Isthmus of Panama, a dream had been realized. A ship could finally sail straight across the continent from the Atlantic to the Pacific.

CHAPTER 11
The Canal Today

Because of the war, the new canal began its life quietly. Afterward, however, it quickly became an important part of the world's economic life. Soon, almost fourteen thousand ships a year were using the canal. Before long, the canal was earning a profit, although the United States had spent so much money that it took until the 1950s to earn it all back.

The canal earns money by charging every ship a toll. The tolls are based on the ship's weight and type, and what cargo it is carrying. So the tolls can vary a good deal. So far the record for the highest toll is $375,600, paid by a cruise ship in 2010. On the other hand, when the athlete Richard Halliburton was allowed to swim the entire canal

in 1928, he was also charged by weight. He had
to pay only thirty-six cents.

The men who designed the Panama Canal
tried to plan for all time. They made the locks as
big as they thought would ever be needed. But no
one had imagined how quickly ships would grow.
In 1936, a ship was built that was too big to fit
into the locks. From then on, anyone shipping
cargo had to decide: did they want the biggest
ship they could have, or did they want to be able

to use the Panama Canal? Most companies that ship a lot of cargo make their ships exactly the largest size that can go through the canal. This size is known as "Panamax."

The number of ships that want to use the canal has also grown steadily. Today there are too many. Only about thirty-five ships a day can pass through the canal. Sometimes there are huge traffic jams at each end as ships wait their turn.

So in 2007, Panama decided to enlarge the canal. They plan to build a third set of locks and widen the passageway so larger ships can get through. Originally they hoped to be finished in time for the canal's hundredth anniversary. Given the history of the Panama Canal, it should be no surprise that there have been unexpected delays. The new Panama Canal is now supposed to open in 2015.

Even before it was finished, the Panama Canal was recognized as being among the greatest human accomplishments ever. In our own time, the American Society of Civil Engineers has named it one of the Seven Wonders of the Modern World. And it inspired one of the world's best-known palindromes. (A palindrome is a sentence that reads the same way from back to front or front to back.) This clever sentence sums up the great achievement neatly: *A man, a plan, a canal: Panama!*

The Canal Zone Is Returned to Panama

Many Panamanians felt that the Americans had forced their way into the country. They hated having an American-controlled canal zone and American military bases in the middle of their country. Over the years, the United States' relationship with Panama

grew more and more tense. Finally, in 1977, President Jimmy Carter agreed to break the treaty that had put the Panama Canal Zone under American control forever. A new treaty was worked out. The United States would have the right to defend the canal if Panama didn't do it properly. In return, control of the canal zone would be given back to the people of Panama. Since noon on December 31, 1999, the canal has been operated by Panama.

Timeline of the Panama Canal

1513	September 25, Balboa becomes the first European to see the Pacific Ocean from the Americas
1846	United States signs a treaty giving it the right to build a path across the Panamanian isthmus
1850	Panama Railroad Company is formed
1855	Panama railroad is completed
1875	An international convention meets in France to discuss building a canal in Panama
1879	French Panama Canal company is formed
1880	January 1, symbolic first shovelful of earth for the canal is dug
1889	The French Panama Canal company goes bankrupt
1903	November 3, Panamanian revolution
	November 6, US officially recognizes the Republic of Panama
1904	In May, US government agrees to buy the bankrupt French company
	In June, construction on the canal is resumed after fifteen years
1905	November 11, the last death from yellow fever in Panama
1913	October 10, the last barrier between the Atlantic and Pacific Oceans is broken through
1914	January 7, the first boat travels through the Panama Canal
	August 15, Panama Canal officially opens
1936	The first ship too big to fit through the Panama Canal is built
1999	The US returns the canal to Panamanian control

Timeline of the World

Ponce de León lands in Florida, becoming the first European to see part of the future United States	1513
Leonardo da Vinci dies	1519
Panama declares its independence from Spain	1821
Gold is discovered in California	1848
Gold miners pour into California	1849
American Civil War begins	1861
May 10, the first transcontinental railroad across North America is completed	1869
November 17, the Suez Canal opens	
Jules Verne publishes *Twenty Thousand Leagues under the Sea*	1870
Invention of the lightbulb	1879
Thomas Stevens rides across North America on a bicycle	1884
Invention of the automobile	1886
United States wins the Philippines and Puerto Rico in the Spanish-American War	1898
President McKinley is assassinated, and Theodore Roosevelt becomes president of the US	1901
December 17, the Wright brothers make the first sustained heavier-than-air airplane flight	1903
San Francisco earthquake destroys much of the city	1906
World War I begins	1914
Colombia recognizes Panamanian independence	1921
The euro is used as money in eleven European countries	1999

Bibliography

*Books for young readers

"American Experience: Panama Canal." PBS. http://www.pbs.org/
   wgbh/americanexperience/films/panama/.

Canal de Panamá. Panama Canal Authority. http://www.pancanal
   .com/eng/.

*DuTemple, Lesley A. *The Panama Canal*. Minneapolis: Lerner,
   2003.

Greene, Julie. *The Canal Builders: Making America's Empire at
   the Panama Canal*. New York: The Penguin Press, 2009.

Keller, Ulrich. *The Building of the Panama Canal in Historic
   Photographs*. New York: Dover Publications, 1983.

McCullough, David. *The Path Between the Seas: The Creation
   of the Panama Canal, 1870–1914*. New York: Simon &
   Schuster, 1977.

Parker, Matthew. *Panama Fever: The Epic Story of One of the
   Greatest Human Achievements of All Time—the Building
   of the Panama Canal*. New York: Doubleday, 2008.